HOME LIBRARY

SHAPING YOUR FIGURE

Printed in the USA.

ISBN: 0-88176-360-8

Cover Design: Jeff Hapner

All of the exercises in this program were developed in consultation with medical experts. However, it is recommended that you consult with your doctor before beginning this, or any, program of exercise.

CONTENTS

YOUR BODY ASSESSMENT

A flat stomach, firm bust and thighs, trim waist and hips—everyone knows what comprises a good figure. And everyone knows why they want one. A trim figure makes you look and feel great. It means you can wear whatever you want to wear without embarrassment. It makes you sexier, more confident, more energetic. It may even make you more employable; studies have shown that employers prefer to hire trim, fit executives and employees.

There's no question that you know what you want and why you want it. The question is how? How do you go about getting a trim, good-looking figure? Until now you've had to hopscotch from one plan or program or book to another. None of them seemed to answer all your questions.

This program will work regardless of your body type, current physical condition, age, or sex. It helps you pinpoint your problem areas. Then it tells you exactly what to do about each of your trouble spots in a detailed step-by-step plan that combines special figure fitness exercises with aerobic activity to put your metabolism into a caloric deficit.

With our plan, all you have to do is do it. And, of course, today, not tomorrow, is the best day to begin this program. Tomorrow symbolizes your good intentions. Tomorrow is every exercise program that we intended to start and that somehow never got off the ground. Think **today** for this program.

Your tailor-made Figure Shaping Program will take only forty-five minutes of your time four days a week. But its rewards will last your entire life. The program will introduce you to a whole new world—one of thinking, doing, and looking your best. There's nothing like looking good and feeling confident. This program will make you feel and look like a million.

YOUR BODY

Consider your amazing body. First, there are the 206 bones of your skeletal system. Your skeleton is the framework of your body; it provides support and protection. Without these bones you would be a blob of tissue.

Attached to your bones are your muscles, all 696 of them. The tug of your muscles on your bones produces action. Walking, lifting, breathing, winking, whistling, yawning, speaking—everything you do is done by the movement of your muscles. These same muscles also shape your body. They shape your chest, waist, legs, and arms, your neck and shoulders and derriere. If these muscles have good tone, if they are strong, firm, and resilient, you will have an attractive, well-formed figure. But, if the muscles lack tone and are underexercised, your breasts, derriere, and thighs will sag. Your arms will be flabby, and your shoulders will droop. Weak and flabby muscles give you a shape, but not the one you want.

To have an attractive figure, you must exercise regularly and vigorously. Muscle strength is vital to your overall health and appearance. Exercise will give you the necessary arm, shoulder, and back strength to maintain correct posture, and it will firm your abdominals to hold in your stomach better than any girdle. But being physically fit does not mean you have to be muscle-bound. Muscle bulkiness in men is caused by the male hormone testosterone. The amount of testosterone present in women is probably too low to have any substantial effect on muscle size; therefore, your body can become strong, firm, and nicely proportioned through exercise without becoming muscle-bound.

Exercise causes muscle fiber to broaden, and it opens new capillaries to feed the muscle. The increased blood supply carries energy and tissue-building materials to the working muscles. Thus, the muscle becomes firmer, more resilient, and toned. In our program, we use exercise to remove flab and tone up muscles. It will give you a figure that you thought was unattainable.

THE NECESSARY FAT

In and around your muscles are deposits of fat. Fat provides insulation and cushioning for the muscles and other organs beneath the muscles. Fat deposits may vary in thickness from a fraction of an inch to several inches, depending on their location, your genetic makeup, and the number of calories you take in and the number of calories you burn each day.

A little body fat is okay. In fact, it's necessary. It enhances

6

certain parts of your figure, e.g., your breasts. But too much fat detracts from your appearance. It gives you bulges and bumps where you don't want them. To remove fat you must burn calories, and the way to burn calories is through physical activity. The champion calorie-burning activities are walking, jogging, bicycling, and swimming. If you do one of these exercises for thirty minutes straight, four or more times a week you will lose body fat.

And what about dieting? When you diet, you may lose weight. But the weight you lose is not necessarily all fat. You may also be losing muscle tissue, the tissue that gives you the luscious and envious figure you desire. Don't diet to lose fat. Exercise it off.

Shaping Your Figure directs you in firming your muscles and in removing body fat. Now, for the first time, you have a design for total figure shaping.

OBESITY

Don't confuse obesity with being overweight. Being overweight means that you weigh more than a person of your height should. A standard height/weight chart may indicate that a 25-year old woman 5 feet tall should weigh about 110 pounds. But such charts are usually based on average heights and weights. No distinction is made as to proportions of bone, muscle, organ, and fat tissue, all of which may vary from person to person. Obesity means having too much body fat. How much fat is too much? As a general guideline, if a woman has 30 percent or more body fat, then she is obese. If a man has 25 percent or more, he is obese.

Let us explain: An overweight woman may be comparatively lean. A gymnast serves as a good example. She may be 5'3" and weigh 138 pounds. According to the height/weight charts, 138 pounds is too much for a woman of her height. Yet, she looks great! How can this be?

The gymnast exercises a lot and is heavily muscled. Much of her body weight is muscle tissue (lean body tissue); only 10 percent of her weight is fat (about 19 percent is the ideal proportion for women). She looks good despite being "overweight." Many athletes—both male and female—are overweight but certainly not obese.

On the other hand, a woman can be obese without being overweight. It is possible to weigh just what the charts say you ought to weigh, but still have a total percentage of body fat that is several points over what is desirable and healthy. Take, for example, a 40-year-old woman who is 5'5" tall and weighs 124 pounds. According to the height/weight charts she is "right on." In fact, her weight may not have changed since she was 21. But she doesn't have the same figure. Her middle and hips have spread. She has jumped a whole dress size. Because she has not had enough exercise, her muscle tissue has given way to fat. Now, 30 percent of her body weight is fat when she should be around 19 percent fat or less.

BODY FAT TESTS

To find out if you have too much body fat, take the following tests.

THE MIRROR TEST

The quickest, easiest way to find out if you are too fat is to get undressed and stand in front of a full-length mirror. Do you like what you see on your body? If you look fat, you are fat. Have your body's contours changed since you were younger, since you changed jobs, since last fall? If your stomach has extra rolls of fat, if your derriere seems flabby, you can conclude that you're too fat. You may be sliding into obesity. Or you may already be there.

THE WEIGHT GAIN TEST

What did you weigh when you were eighteen? If memory fails, dig out old medical records. You can assume that each pound gained since that time represents a one-pound accumulation of fat, not lean body tissue. If you've gained five pounds or more, you can conclude that you're moving into the obese range.

CHEST/WAIST MEASUREMENT

Stand with your shoulders pulled back and your chest fully expanded. Measure the circumference of your chest just below your armpits, making sure that your tape measure is flat and level. Then, with your abdomen in a relaxed position (not sucked in or forced out), measure your waist at your navel. Your chest circumference should be ten inches larger (or more) than that of your waist.

If your chest is not ten inches greater than your waist, there's probably too much fat on your abdomen.

THE PINCH TEST

Using only your thumb and forefinger, try to grasp the skin and fat anywhere on your body. Try your waist, derriere, arm, chest, thigh, or calf. If you pinch more than one inch, you have too much body fat.

The mirror, weight gain, chest/waist, and pinch tests are an indication of how much body fat you're carrying. If these tests indicate that you carry too much fat, you're not burning off enough calories to compete with the number of calories you eat, and you must do calorie-burning exercises.

MUSCLE TONE TESTS
PUSH-UP TEST

Lie flat on the floor, face down. Place your hands directly under your shoulders. Keep your legs straight, and curl your toes under slightly. Slowly push yourself upward until your arms are straight, then lower yourself back to the starting position. Do as many as possible up to ten. If you are unable to do ten push-ups, the muscles of your arms and shoulders are not adequately toned.

SIT-UP TEST

Lie on the floor with your knees bent and your feet on the floor in front of you. Your hands should be grasped behind your neck. Now slowly curl yourself up until your elbows touch your knees, and then return to the starting position. Do as many as possible up to ten. If you cannot do ten sit-ups, your abdominal muscles are too weak.

WALL SIT TEST

Stand about eighteen inches from a wall, toes pointed straight ahead. Now lean your upper body, lower back, and derriere against the wall. Your arms should hang at your sides. Slowly bend your knees and slide your hips downward until your thighs are parallel to the floor. Hold for ten seconds.

If you are unable to hold this position for ten seconds, your leg muscles are weak and untoned.

If you have done poorly on these tests, your problem is a lack of muscle development and you must do muscle-strengthening exercises.

HOW HEREDITY AFFECTS YOUR FIGURE

People come in different shapes and sizes: big ones, small ones, fat ones, skinny ones, short ones, and tall ones. Bone structure, the number of fibers in the muscles, the length of the intestines, and a host of other genetic factors play a major role in the way you look.

For years, scientists have tried to classify people according to their inherited body type. One of the most common methods of classification is somatotyping, through which the human body can be classified into three basic types by estimating the balance of fat, muscle, and bone.

Briefly, somatotyping divides human bodies into endomorphs, mesomorphs, and ectomorphs. An endomorph has a round or soft body with little muscle development and small bones. Her weight is centered in the front of her body around the abdomen. She usually does poorly in athletic events that require support of her body, speed, agility, endurance, or jumping. She may excel only in sports like golf, archery, or swimming.

If you are an endomorph, it may be difficult for you to lose all the apparent flab on your body. You are prone to putting on fat and retaining fat once it is gained. You will probably always look a little heavier than your ectomorphic or mesomorphic friends. Your problem is complicated by the fact that you are successful at so few big calorie-burning activities. Swimming is perhaps your one true fat-burning exercise.

Don't be discouraged if you're an endomorph. But, understand your limitations. You will make progress using the Figure Shaping Program, but it may be slow. And you may not achieve an "ideal" figure. Fortunately, very few people fall into this extreme category. Most people who think they're endomorphs are really mesomorphs who are trying to find an excuse for being in bad shape.

A mesomorph is muscular and big-boned. She is noted for hardness and ruggedness. Normally she is of moderate height with a long neck and broad shoulders. A mesomorph has a large chest, a relatively slender waist, and broad hips. Mesomorphs usually excel in practically all physical activities. We've got good news and bad news for the mesomorphs. First the bad news: Mesomorphs have a tendency to put on weight after giving up sports. They develop the classic middle-age spread. Now for the good news: Once they return to a bona fide exercise program they make rapid improvements. They lose fat quickly, and their muscles firm up rapidly.

An ectomorph is thin-muscled and thin-boned. She looks fragile and delicate. Ectomorphs have the classic fashion model's body: short trunk and long neck and limbs. They have very little body fat. Generally, however, ectomorphs have poor posture because they lack muscular strength and proper support. They excel in activities such as badminton, tennis, and endurance running. Traditional muscle-strengthening calisthenics often produce striking results for ectomorphs.

Of course, most of us do not fall into any of these extreme categories. There are very few endomorphs, mesomorphs, or ectomorphs. Each of us simply has a tendency toward fatness, muscularity, or thinness.

You should decide which tendency you have. Are you more of an ectomorph, a mesomorph, or an endomorph? Once you know your body type, you will know what kind of work is cut out for you and what kind of results you can expect from the Figure Shaping Program.

• If there is a tendency in your family toward obesity (your mother and father tended to be fat), you can conclude you are on the endomorphic side. If that's the case, expect your results to be less dramatic than those of the mesomorph.

• If at one time you had a good physique, but lately some parts have sagged and spread, you're probably a mesomorph. Lucky for you. You will see dramatic changes with the Figure Shaping Program.

• If your family tends toward thinness, you're probably an ectomorph. You'll find the exercises in the Figure Shaping Program effective in building your figure, although the process will take you a little longer than it would a mesomorph.

YOUR ASSESSMENT

The best way to see your fitness needs clearly is to summarize and record them in one spot. The following summary will help you establish your goals and will serve as a reference point for gauging your progress.

Answer the questions listed here. Then use your answers to set up a chart like the one following the questions.

(Circle One)

1. Are you displeased with the appearance of your body as you look in a full-length mirror?

   Yes   No

2. Is your chest less than ten inches larger than your waistline?

   Yes   No

3. Have you gained more than five pounds since you were eighteen years of age?

   Yes   No

4. Can you pinch more than one inch of fat anywhere on your body?

   Yes   No

   Where? (Circle Body Area)
   Arms   Hips
   Shoulders   Thighs
   Abdomen   Calf
   Waist

5. How did you do on the Muscle Tone Tests?

   (Circle One)
   a. Did you pass the Push-Up Test?   Yes   No
   b. Did you pass the Sit-Up Test?   Yes   No
   c. Did you pass the Wall Sit Test? Yes   No

If you answered any of the first four questions (especially the Pinch Test) **yes,** your problem is too much fat. In that case you must engage in calorie-burning exercises such as walking, bicycling, swimming, or jogging a minimum of thirty minutes four or more times a week. That will get your body into caloric balance and will help you lose body fat.

If you answered **no** to any of the questions listed under #5, your problem is muscle weakness. That means you'll have to do our program of muscle-strengthening exercise.

Furthermore, if you answered **yes** to the first four questions and **no** to those listed under #5 you have both weak muscles and too much fat. Therefore, you must engage in a program that burns a significant number of calories and at the same time conditions different muscle groups. Now take this information and jot down what you've learned from these questions. Make a list like the one below and keep it handy for reference.

Pretest

Date _____   My Goals
Number of Push-Ups _____   _____
Number of Sit-Ups_____   _____
Number of Seconds Wall Sit_____   _____

Sizes
(in inches,
where applicable)

		Satisfied?	
Shoulders	_____	Yes	No
Arms	_____	Yes	No
Forearms	_____	Yes	No
Chest	_____	Yes	No
Waist/Abdomen	_____	Yes	No
Hips	_____	Yes	No
Thighs	_____	Yes	No
Calves	_____	Yes	No
Ankles	_____	Yes	No

Pinch test	Can You Pinch An Inch?	
Chest	Yes	No
Waist/Abdomen	Yes	No
Hips	Yes	No
Thighs	Yes	No
Derriere	Yes	No

Perform this test before you begin the Figure Shaping Program. Repeat the test after you've been in the program one week, twelve weeks, and twenty-four weeks. You should see definite changes.

YOUR FIGURE SHAPING PROGRAM

No one has a perfect figure for all of their life. As you age, your hips spread. Your bustline sags. Your abdomen looks pudgy. You can't stop the process of aging, but you can slow down the loss of your figure.

The Figure Shaping Program will firm up your problem areas with muscle-toning exercise and it will burn off excess fat with aerobic activity. The program will take you about forty-five minutes four times a week, and it will be worth every minute of it. You will look better, and you'll feel better and have more energy.

This is a three-level, eighteen-stage program. Try to do the entire workout of exercises and fat-burning activity in one session. If you can't spare forty-five minutes at once, remember that it is better to do the workout in two sessions than it is not to exercise at all.

No matter how fit you are, start this plan at Level One. Spend at least one week at each stage unless you find the workout exceptionally easy. If so, you can move to the next stage. On the other hand, if you find Stage One taxing, stay there until your body calls for more exercise.

How quickly you move through these levels depends upon your body's own demands and changes. You can stay at a particular stage if you are satisfied with your figure change. If your body seems to rebel at too high a level of exercise, back off a bit. Learn to listen to your body. If it seems to be telling you that you've had enough, respect it.

We have structured the program to help you improve both your muscle tone and your body fat percentage, but you must understand that your body may be ready for Stage Three of the muscle-toning exercises and for only Stage Two of the fat-burning exercises. If so, don't worry. Progress at a rate that you feel is in line with your ability. Eventually you'll reach

Stage Eighteen of both the fat-burning and the muscle-toning exercises.

PROGRAM POINTERS

1. Don't push yourself too hard. You didn't become soft and flabby overnight. It took time. Restoration also takes time. If you approach your program too vigorously, you may show fast progress at first, but you're soon going to get sore and discouraged, and you may decide to quit. If you follow the program as outlined, you'll keep your aches and pains minimal. You'll progress gradually and painlessly. Follow the guidelines we have built into this program, and don't force yourself to go faster.

In this program we do not specify a certain number of repetitions for each exercise. Rather, you are told to do the exercise for a specified number of seconds. Thus, each person can do the number of repetitions commensurate with her ability. Try to do as many repetitions as possible in the time allotted. But do not do so many that you are exhausted and unable to do the next exercise.

2. Exercise on a comfortable surface. Try to exercise on a mat. Most floor exercises can irritate your tailbone or hipbones. The skin over your tailbone, for example, may get rubbed raw by the constant friction against the floor. If you don't have a mat to sit on, a towel folded four times will do. A carpet remnant or a piece of foam rubber will also work.

3. Avoid exercises that may be harmful. Unfortunately, many fitness books recommend several exercises which can do more harm than good.

Straight Leg Sit-Ups—sit-ups done with the ankles held down and the legs straight are not beneficial in toning your abdomen. The hip flexors, or the iliopsoas muscle (the muscle that runs from the spinal column to the thigh bone), do most of the work when you do straight leg sit-ups. Continuing to do this exercise will result in a shortening of the muscles in the lower back and thighs.

If you bend your knees when doing a sit-up, you place all the stress on the abdominal muscles and immobilize the hip flexors, thus toning the abdomen and avoiding back pain.

One more important point: When doing sit-ups, do them in a curling motion, thereby adding to the stress on your abdominal region and reducing trauma to the lower back area.

Toe Touches—toe touching does not trim the waistline. Gravity, not your abdominal muscles, pulls you down toward your feet. Toe touching strengthens and sometimes aggravates the muscles of the lower back. In addition, the action of bending forward and bouncing to touch the toes forces the knees to overextend and places tremendous amounts of pressure on the lumbar vertebrae, a factor believed by many to result in low back complaints.

Leg Lifts—to do leg lifts, you lie on your back and lift your legs six inches off the floor. Leg lifts can increase the severity of low back pain because the abdominal muscles usually aren't strong enough to hold your legs off the floor for any length of time. Therefore, when you raise your legs, you are unable to keep your low back on the floor. As a result, there is a forward rotation of the pelvis which can aggravate a pain of the lower back.

Back Body Arches—exercises that involve arching the back are sometimes done to strengthen the lower back muscles. The problem is that the lower back tends to be a lot stronger than the abdominal muscles and that by arching the back, you will strengthen the lower back even more and stretch the abdominals. Thus, arching the back increases the muscle imbalance and causes greater distress to the low back.

Deep Knee Bends—deep knee bends stretch the lateral ligaments of the knee. Excessive stretching all but eliminates the natural protection of the knee. Deep knee bends (that is, sitting all the way down on your haunches) and duck walk activities almost universally have been condemned by exercise physiologists, but not all knee bends are dangerous. "Full knee bends" or "deep knee bends" refer to those in which the buttocks touch the heels of the feet. You can do knee bends safely as long as you squat only to the point where the thighs are parallel to the floor and eliminate completely the duck waddle and all bouncing movements.

A Special Note: Some of our exercises call for the use of barbells, dumbbells, or shoe weights. Weights can be purchased inexpensively from many department and sporting goods stores. You can substitute common household items for most of these props if they are unavailable or you do not wish to purchase them. Two large-size tomato juice cans (with juice of course) or two heavy, dictionary-size books can substitute for the dumbbells. If you have no shoe weight, try wearing a heavy hiking boot when you do the exercises that ask for a weighted shoe.

To gauge whether your weights are heavy enough, try lifting them ten times in succession. If you can easily lift them ten times or more, you should be using heavier weights. You will probably have to add more weight every two to three weeks as you progress through the program and as your muscles become stronger.

Some exercises call for a rope. The rope should be an eight- or nine-foot length of non-irritating, non-stretchy material. A washline or a jump rope without handles would work well.

HOW TO USE THE MUSCLE-TONING EXERCISES

You'll find a series of exercises in this book for eight different body areas. Each set of exercises (except those for the lower back) is divided by level of difficulty into three groups—beginning, intermediate, and advanced. You are to move from one level of difficulty to the next when you feel ready for a more demanding level of activity.

Once you have identified your basic figure problems, you can select the exercises which are best for you and your figure. Your program may involve one body part or several, and you are to do the beginning level exercises for those parts of your body that need the most work. For example, if your abdomen, waist, and hips are your three problem areas, you are to do the four beginning level exercises for each of those areas. The abdomen would include the head and shoulder curl, single leg raises (knee bent), double knee raise, and curl-downs. The four exercises for the waist would be the single side leg raises, double knee lifts, crossovers, and the side curl-ups. And the four beginning exercises for the hips would be the standing leg extensions, the side leg swings, the side stretch, and the double knee lifts. You will perform each of these twelve exercises for five to ten seconds four or five times a week (see chart in this chapter). When you feel ready, you can progress to Stage Two, where you will do exercises for eleven to fifteen seconds. Move to the next stage when your body seems to demand more exercise. When you have completed Stage Six of Level One, you are ready to move on to Level Two.

Level One is your introduction to a better figure. In Level Two the workouts become more demanding as you progress to the intermediate exercises. Continue to work through the stages of Level Two at your own pace, progressing as the workouts become easier by doing each exercise for a longer time.

When the Stage Twelve workout is no longer demanding, you'll progress to Level Three and the advanced exercises for your trouble spots. Progress through Level Three in the same way you have progressed through the earlier levels.

If you are not satisfied with your figure when you reach Level Three, Stage Eighteen (and it could happen), you have two alternatives. You can make your workout longer by adding minutes or seconds to the routine. For example, after Stage Eighteen (Level Three) you could do the exercises for forty-six to sixty seconds.

Or, if you prefer, try to work faster; do more repetitions in the specified period of time. For example, if you reach Level Three, Stage Eighteen and you're doing twenty sit-ups in forty-five seconds, you might strive to do twenty-five sit-ups in forty-five seconds.

THE FAT-BURNING ACTIVITIES

In addition to muscle-toning exercises, the Figure Shaping Program includes fat-burning activities. It is important to do this part of the workout whether or not your body assessment indicated that you have too high a percentage of body fat. Do not neglect the fat-burners even if you are an ectomorph!

Whereas most of us will start doing the fat-burners primarily to lose excess body fat, fat-burning or aerobic activity has other very important benefits as well. Perhaps its most important benefit is that it will introduce (or reintroduce) us to an active life. Most figure problems can be traced to our sedentary lifestyle. Weak muscles, poor posture, flabby midsections—all are usually due, in part or whole, to lack of activity. The fat-burning part of the Figure Shaping Program is graduated so that your body can readjust to the increasing demands made upon it—the rest of your workout, i.e. the muscle-toning exercises, will become easier, not only because you are strengthening your muscles but because the fat-burners are teaching your lungs and heart to work harder.

At the beginning level, our suggested fat-burning activity is walking. As you work through the six stages of Level One, you will walk for a longer period of time. At Level Two you will walk for a period, then walk/run for a brief period; and with each stage you will run for a longer time. At Level Three you will be running for a longer time than you will be walking.

Try to do your fat-burning activity immediately after your muscle-toning exercises. Do not take a leisurely stroll through the house and call that your walk. Go outside and take a brisk walk through your neighborhood. Try not to pause in your walk. Keep moving. It is long continuous movement that burns fat.

YOUR FIGURE SHAPING PROGRAM

The following chart will tell you how long to perform each of the exercises in your personal figure shaping plan. Don't forget to do warm-up and cool-down exercises before and after your muscle-toning exercises.

Level One	Stage One	Stage Two	Stage Three	Stage Four	Stage Five	Stage Six
Warm-Up Exercises*	5	5	5	5 minutes	5	5
Beginning Level Muscle-Toning Exercises	5-10	11-15	16-20	21-25 seconds	26-30	30-40
Fat Burner: Walk	15-16	17-19	20-22	23-25 minutes	26-29	30
Cool-Down Exercises*	5	5	5	5 minutes	5	5

Level Two	Stage Seven	Stage Eight	Stage Nine	Stage Ten	Stage Eleven	Stage Twelve
Warm-Up Exercises*	5	5	5	5 minutes	5	5
Intermediate Level Muscle-Toning Exercises	15-20	21-25	26-30	31-35 seconds	36-40	41-45
Fat Burner: Walk	5	5	5	5 minutes	5	5
Run	15-16	17-19	20-22	23-25 minutes	26-28	29-30
Cool-Down Exercises*	5	5	5	5 minutes	5	5

*See Appendix for Warm-Up and Cool-Down Exercises

Level Three	Stage Thirteen	Stage Fourteen	Stage Fifteen	Stage Sixteen	Stage Seventeen	Stage Eighteen
Warm-Up Exercises*	5	5	5 minutes	5	5	5
Advanced Level Muscle-Toning Exercises	15-20	21-25	26-30 seconds	31-35	36-40	41-45
Fat Burner: Walk	15	15	15 minutes	15	15	15
Run	3	4-6	7-9 minutes	10-12	11-14	15
Cool-Down Exercises*	5	5	5 minutes	5	5	5

*See Appendix for Warm-Up and Cool-Down Exercises

SHOULDER & UPPER BACK EXERCISES

"What do the shoulders and upper back have to do with figure fitness?" you may be asking yourself. "After all, the bosom, waist, hips, and legs are what count." And it is true that well-toned shoulders may not seem as obvious a figure asset as a flat stomach or firm thighs. But the benefits provided by the following exercises are multiple. They'll help prevent or alleviate figure problems like rounded shoulders. They'll tone the muscles to give you a well-conditioned, rather than bony, shoulder line. And they'll strengthen the muscles of the upper back to improve your carriage and posture.

Rounded shoulders droop forward because the upper back muscles are not strong enough to hold the upper body upright. The condition is a double loss; when you slouch, your bustline looks smaller than it is and your breasts sag.

The short, thick muscle that caps the shoulder is called the deltoid. The deltoid helps to raise the arm and move it backward and forward. This muscle is both visible and very attractive when kept in proper shape.

Muscles of the upper back include the trapezius, the supraspinatus, the infraspinatus, and the teres major and minor. While only the kite-shaped trapezius is visible, all these muscles are crucial to your posture and carriage. Strengthening them will help you carry yourself with poise and confidence.

GIANT ARM CIRCLES
(BEGINNING LEVEL)

1. Stand erect, feet shoulder-width apart, arms at your sides.

2. Swing both your arms in giant circles.

3. Continue for the specified number of seconds.

HIGH ARM SWINGS

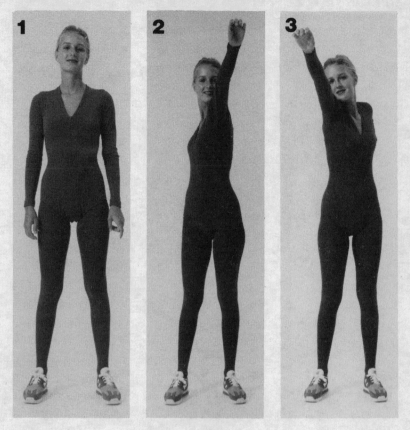

1. Stand with arms at your sides.

2. Swing your arms alternately forward and back. The hands should reach shoulder height on the forward swing.

3. Do for the specified number of seconds.

SHOULDER ROLL

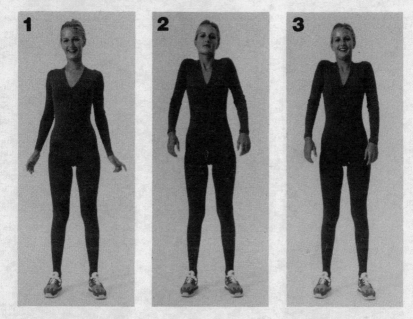

1. Stand with arms at sides.

2. Rotate the shoulders upward, back, and down, keeping the arms relaxed. Use only the muscles of the upper back and shoulders.

3. Do for the specified number of seconds.

ARM EXTENSIONS OVERHEAD

1. Stand with arms at sides.

2. Reach upward; clasp the hands, and push your arms backward.

3. Draw both hands down in front of your chest, and flex the arms.

4. Do for the specified number of seconds.

DOORWAY PRESS
(INTERMEDIATE LEVEL)

1. Stand in the center of a doorway, feet comfortably apart. Place your palms against the doorway jambs so that your arms are fully extended above the head.

2. Press with both hands against the edges of the doorway. Be certain to keep the body straight. Hold for a few seconds. Relax.

3. Do for the specified number of seconds.

Note: The exercise can be modified by placing the hands at shoulder height with the arms bent.

BACKWARD RAISE

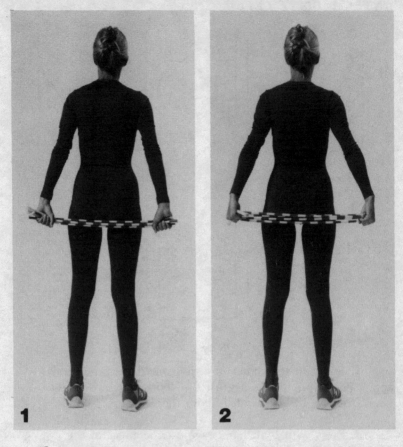

1. Loop the rope twice; hold it behind your buttocks.

2. With the palms of your hands turned in toward your thighs, grasp the rope and pull outward and away from your body.

3. Hold for a few seconds. Relax.

4. Do for the specified number of seconds.

ARM EXTENDER

1. Loop the rope; hold it in front of your chest with your arms extended outward, parallel to the floor.

2. Exerting a pull outward, stretch the rope until it is taut. Hold for a few seconds.

3. Relax. Do for the specified number of seconds.

MODIFIED PUSH-UPS

1. Lie face down, hands on the floor beneath the shoulders, fingers pointed forward, and knees bent.

2. Lift your body (from the knees up) off the floor by straightening the arms. Keep your back straight.

3. Return to the starting position. Do for the specified number of seconds.

SHOULDER SHRUG
(ADVANCED LEVEL)

1. Stand with feet apart. Hold barbell in overhand grip against thighs.

2. Lift your shoulders; try to touch the top of your shoulders to your ears.

3. Lower your shoulders slowly to the original position. Do for the specified number of seconds.

LATERAL RAISE

1. Stand with feet slightly apart. Hold dumbbells at the sides of your body in overhand grip.

2. Lift dumbbells sideways to a horizontal level—or beyond, if you comfortably can, to an overhead position.

3. Return to the starting position. Do for the specified number of seconds.

PRONE ARM LIFT

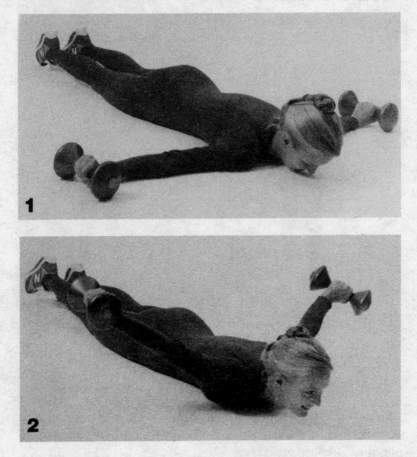

1. Assume a prone position on the floor; arms extended at right angles to the body. Grasp the dumbbells with overhand grip.

2. Raise arms as high as possible toward the ceiling.

3. Lower arms slowly back to the original position. Do for the specified number of seconds.

ARM PRESS

1. Stand with feet apart.

2. Hold barbell at chest level, using overhand grip.

3. Extend the barbell over the head, straightening the arms.

4. Return the barbell to the starting position. Do for the specified number of seconds.

ARM EXERCISES

Many women worry about developing flabby, unsightly arms. They recall seeing their mothers and grandmothers with what appeared to be ponderous accumulations of fat on the backside of their arms. As they get older, and their own arms begin to lose tone and firmness, they try to hide this unattractive feature by wearing long-sleeved dresses and blouses.

Many people believe that this unsightly condition is due to fat deposits. In fact, the flabby appearance is most often due to weak muscles. When people squeeze the back of the arm to feel their fat, in reality they may be squeezing a muscle (the triceps brachii) which has become so weak and flabby that it feels like fat!

A flabby triceps results from disuse. American women rarely participate in pushing activities. They lift the clothes basket, their children, typewriters, furniture, and briefcases. But the modern American female (or male for that matter) seldom pushes a car out of the mud. How many of us even use a nonmotorized lawn mower? And flabbiness is the result of not using muscles at the back of the arm. Fortunately, this muscle responds quickly to proper exercise.

Conversely, if your arms are too thin, proper exercise will go a long way toward getting them in proper proportion.

Your arm and wrist muscles also affect your figure. These long, slim muscles extend up your arm and through your shoulders. No matter how attractive your figure is, if your arms and wrists are flabby and weak or thin and bony, people will notice.

ARM FLEX
(BEGINNING LEVEL)

1. Stand with your feet apart and the arms extended to the sides at shoulder height. Palms should be up.

2. Flex the arms inward as though making a muscle. Touch your fingertips to your shoulders.

3. Return to starting position. Repeat for the specified number of seconds.

PUNCHING BAG

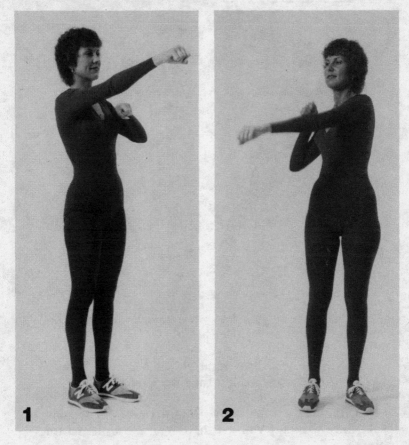

1. Simulate punching a punching bag with the arms alternately extended and flexed.

2. You can put variety into this workout by twisting at the waist as you move your arms from left to right.

3. Continue for the specified number of seconds.

WALL PUSH-UP

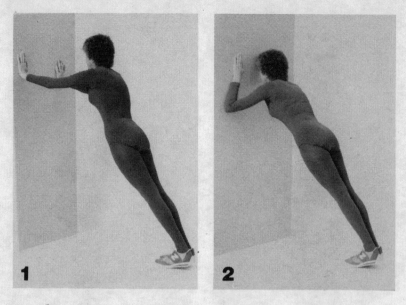

1. Stand about three feet away from a wall. Place both hands on the wall at shoulder height.

2. Keeping your body rigid, slowly bend your arms and touch your chin to the wall. (Take three seconds.)

3. Push away from the wall until your arms are straight. (Take three seconds.) You will have returned to the starting point.

4. Repeat for the specified number of seconds.

REACH BACK

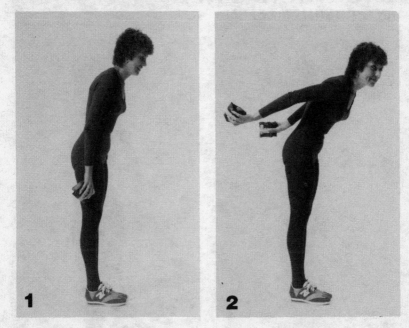

1. Stand with the trunk inclined forward at a 45° angle, arms at your sides. Hold a small weight in each hand.

2. Make sure your arms are straight, shoulders back, and your elbows locked. Push your arms backward and upward as high as possible. Hold for a few seconds.

3. Relax. Repeat for the specified number of seconds.

BACKWARD PULL
(INTERMEDIATE LEVEL)

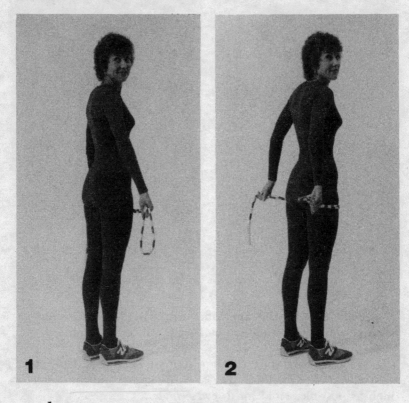

1. Grasp a rope, and hold it in front of you at about hip level. Your arms should be at your sides, palms turned backward.

2. Keeping your arms straight, pull the ends of the rope backward and upward. Hold for three seconds. Relax.

3. Repeat for the specified number of seconds.

BACKWARD RAISE

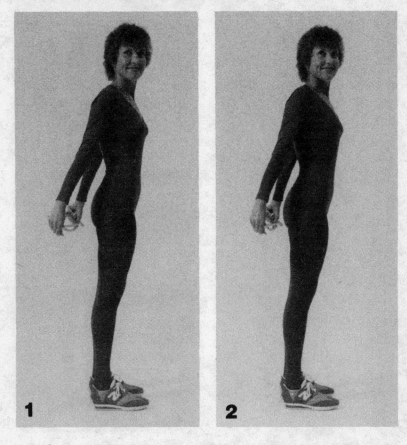

1. Loop the rope twice, and hold it behind the back.

2. With the palms of your hands turned in toward your thighs, pull the rope outward and away from your body. Hold for three seconds. Relax.

3. Repeat for the specified number of seconds.

CURL

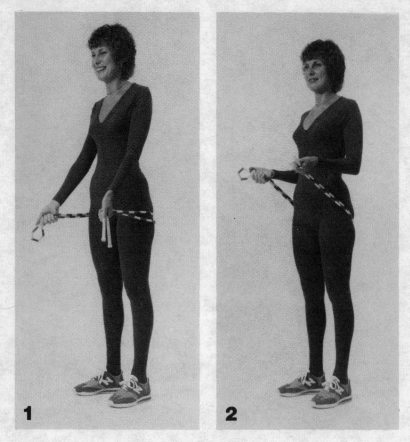

1. Hold the rope behind you, under your buttocks. Grasp the rope with palms turned upward.

2. Keeping your elbows at your sides, with your arms bent at a 90° angle, exert a force upward. Hold for three seconds. Relax.

3. Repeat for the specified number of seconds.

CHARLIE ATLAS

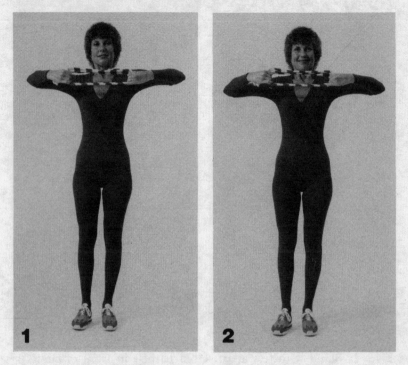

1. Loop the rope twice, and hold it in front of your chest with palms turned in toward your body.

2. Keeping your hands as close to your chest as possible, pull the rope outward with your arms until it is taut. Hold for three seconds. Relax.

3. Repeat for the specified number of seconds.

ARM PRESS
(ADVANCED LEVEL)

1. Stand with feet apart. Hold barbell in front of chest, using overhand grip.

2. Extend the barbell over the head, straightening the arms. Return to the starting position.

3. Repeat for the specified number of seconds.

BENCH PRESS

1. Lie on a bench; knees bent, feet flat on the floor. Hold barbell across chest, overhand grip.

2. Press barbell upward until arms are fully extended. Return barbell slowly to starting position.

3. Repeat for the specified number of seconds.

BARBELL CURLS

1. Stand with feet shoulder-width apart, arms at sides. Hold barbell against the thighs in underhand grip.

2. Flex forearms, raising barbell to shoulders. Return to the starting position.

3. Repeat for the specified number of seconds.

TRICEPS PRESS

1. Stand with feet apart, holding dumbbells overhead.

2. Lower dumbbells slowly behind neck, bending elbows (as the weight is brought down toward the shoulder, the elbows will tend to point toward the ceiling). Return to starting position.

3. Repeat for the specified number of seconds.

CHEST & BUSTLINE EXERCISES

Physicians long ago concluded that the bustline of almost any normal female can be enhanced through the right type of exercise. A buildup of the muscles that lie under the breasts and an increase in overall chest expansion can improve your appearance automatically. Add the important benefits to be derived from postural reeducation, and you could look like a different woman.

These exercises will broaden the fibers of the pectoral muscles and open new capillaries to feed the muscles. The increased blood supply will carry energy and tissue-building materials to the working muscles. Protein will be carried and utilized for new tissue growth; and fats, also carried in the bloodstream, may be deposited between the muscle fibers as well as under the skin and over the muscle. In this way, a new natural form takes shape without disturbing or irritating these delicate glands.

The key muscle to be developed in a chest improvement program is the pectoralis major. Large and fan-like, the pectoralis major covers the upper part of the chest and gathers to join the deltoid (the muscle which caps the shoulder). You can actually feel the pectoralis major. While standing or sitting, raise your left arm sideways to shoulder level. Place your right hand on the left side of your chest above the breast so that your fingertips touch the lower border of your left shoulder or the upper part of your chest. Now move your left arm forward. You should be able to feel the pectoralis major bunch up under your fingers.

There are three other chest muscles. The pectoralis minor lies beneath the pectoralis major. This muscle moves the shoulder forward, downward, and away from your body and raises the third, fourth, and fifth ribs when you take a deep breath. The subclavius, a small cylindrical muscle located between the shoulder blade and the first rib, moves your shoulder forward and downward. The fourth chest muscle, the serratus anterior, lies between your ribs and shoulder blade. The serratus anterior rotates the shoulder blade, bends and straightens the arms, and aids in pushing.

Regular exercise will build up all these muscles. Those of you who play handball, tennis, badminton, or squash will get an added benefit from a chest exercise program. Stronger chest muscles will help improve your arm swings.

Developing these muscles will improve a small or sagging bustline. Amply endowed women will not reduce their bustline by strengthening their pectoral muscles. Only aerobic exercise will help them by reducing the amount of fat in the fat cells of the breasts.

FOREARM PRESS
(BEGINNING LEVEL)

1. In a sitting or standing position, hold the left forearm across the body at chin level; bend your arm at the elbow so that the palm is facing toward the chest.

2. Place your right hand on the forearm of your left arm and your left hand on the forearm of your right arm.

3. Push vigorously against your forearms.

4. Repeat for the specified number of seconds.

ARM PRESS

2

1. Stand. Hold your hands at chest level.

2. Place the fist of one hand in the palm of the other.

3. Push fist and palm against each other.

4. Reverse hands. Alternate for the specified number of seconds.

WALL PUSH-UP

1. Stand about three feet away from a wall. Place both hands on the wall at shoulder height.

2. Keeping your body rigid, slowly bend your arms and touch your chin to the wall. (Take three seconds.)

3. Return to starting position. (Take three seconds.)

4. Repeat for the specified number of seconds.

BENT ARM PULLOVERS

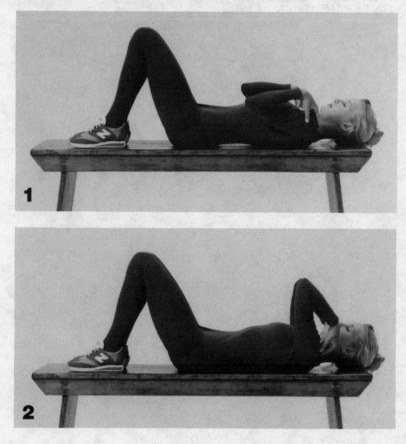

1. Lie on a bench, elbows bent, arms beside your body, fingertips touching the shoulders.

2. Lift your elbows, moving them as far as possible. As you do this your hands will slip below your shoulders.

3. Return to the starting position, and repeat for the specified number of seconds.

ARMS OVER
(INTERMEDIATE LEVEL)

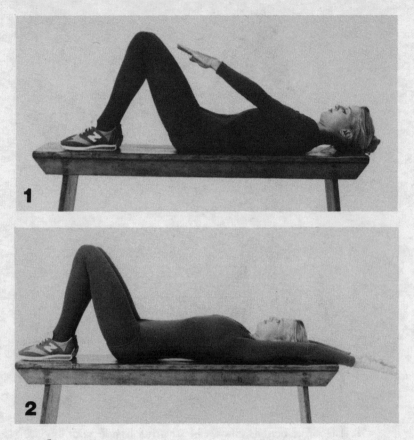

1. Lie on a bench, knees bent. Extend arms toward your knees.

2. Draw your arms over your head reaching as far back as possible, making an arc. Hold for a few seconds, and return to the starting position.

3. Do for the specified number of seconds.

RIGHT ANGLES

1. Lie on a bench with your arms at right angles to your body, knees bent, feet on the bench. Hold a weight in each hand.

2. Raise your arms so they point straight up.

3. Return to the starting position. Do for the specified number of seconds.

MODIFIED PUSH-UP

1. Start in a lying position, hands beneath your shoulders, fingers pointed forward, knees bent.

2. Lift your body (from the knees up) off the floor by straightening your arms. Keep your back straight.

3. Return to the starting position. Repeat for the specified number of seconds.

BENCH PRESS

1. Lie on a bench, knees bent, feet flat on the floor. Hold barbell across the chest, overhand grip.

2. Press barbell upward until arms are fully extended.

3. Return barbell slowly to starting position. Repeat for the specified number of seconds.

SUPINE PULLOVER
(ADVANCED LEVEL)

1. Lie on your back. Hold barbell on floor above head with overhand grip.

2. Raise arms to a 90° angle directly overhead; keep arms straight.

3. Return barbell to original position, keeping arms straight.

4. Repeat for the specified number of seconds.

THE BARREL

1. Lie on a bench, knees bent, feet on bench. Hold two weights, placing your arms as far apart as possible.

2. Bring the weights together above your chest. Keep arms bent as though you were holding a barrel.

3. Return to the starting position, and repeat for the specified number of seconds.

REGULAR PUSH-UPS

1. Lie face down on the floor, feet together, hands beneath your shoulders.

2. Keeping your body straight, lift your body off the floor by extending your arms fully. Then return to the starting position.

3. Do for the specified number of seconds.

BENCH PRESS

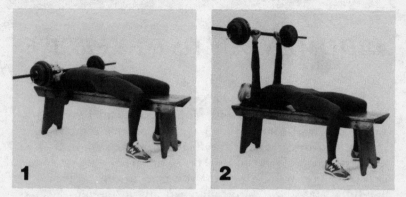

1. Lie on a bench, knees bent, feet flat on the floor. Hold the barbell across chest, overhand grip.

2. Press barbell upward until arms are fully extended.

3. Return barbell slowly to starting position. Do for the specified number of seconds.

ABDOMEN & WAIST EXERCISES

You have a natural girdle that's more effective and comfortable than anything any girdle manufacturer ever contrived. It will control your waistline, provide complete freedom of movement, and it will never, never ride up or down, causing you embarrassment. It can relieve you of lower back pain, give you the support you need to carry yourself gracefully, and it will adjust automatically to the muscle stress of pregnancy and childbirth. Mother Nature has equipped you with a true "24-hour girdle" that is so comfortable that you "won't believe it's a girdle." This natural girdle is composed of the muscles of your abdomen.

Four groups of muscles make up your abdominal girdle. Each group is actually a pair of muscles—one on the right side of your abdomen and one on the left. The rectus abdominis muscles run vertically from the middle of your rib cage to your pubic bone. If you have a little pot belly, that's a clue your rectus abdominis muscles are out of shape. If you have a big pot belly, all of your stomach muscles are out of shape.

The external and internal oblique muscles run on an angle from your ribs to your hips and help hold the organs of your abdomen in place.

The transverse muscles run horizontally. They start behind the rectus abdominis muscles and extend to the hips, backbone, and ribs. Their main function is to help hold the contents of the abdominal cavity in place. The transverse and oblique muscles, if unexercised, will make the waist wider. All these muscles form the crosshatch of your natural girdle. These are the muscles that give shape to your waist, support the organs of your abdominal cavity, squeeze the contents of your stomach and intestines during digestion, protect your internal organs from blows, and keep your pelvis in its proper position. When unexercised, these muscles can provide little support, and every one of those functions is impaired.

Generally, when we talk about the stomach we are referring to the area beneath the rib cage and above the pubic region. We have divided these exercises into two areas: the abdomen and the waist. We have defined the abdomen as that area in front of your body near the navel and the waist as that area on the sides of your abdomen or stomach region. People who have a pot belly or a spare tire need to exercise the abdominal region. Someone with love-handles or flabby sides has a waist problem and should do our waist exercises.

HEAD AND SHOULDER CURL
(BEGINNING LEVEL—ABDOMEN)

1. Lie on your back with your knees bent at a 90° angle, feet on the floor, arms crossed on your chest. (You may, instead, place your hands behind your neck or place your arms along the sides of your body.)

2. Tighten your abdominal muscles. Roll your head and shoulders up off the floor. Hold.

3. Return to the starting position. Do for the specified number of seconds.

SINGLE LEG RAISE
(KNEE BENT)

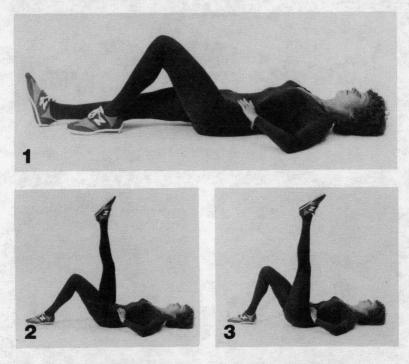

1. Lie on your back with your left knee bent and your left foot on the floor. Extend your right leg along the floor, and place your hands on your hips or at your sides.

2. Raise your right leg as high as possible, keeping the small of your back against the floor. Return your right leg to the floor.

3. Do the exercise with the right leg for half the specified number of seconds, then do the exercise with your left leg for half the specified number of seconds.

DOUBLE KNEE RAISE

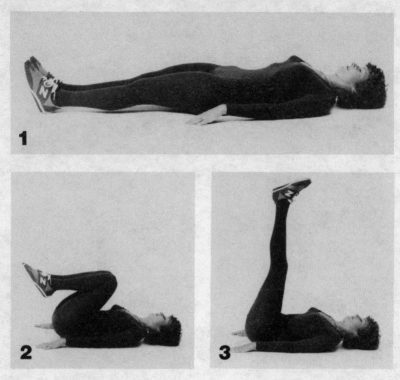

1. Lie on your back with your legs straight out on the floor, arms at your sides.

2. Bring both knees up as close to your chest as possible. Keep the small of your back against the floor.

3. Extend both legs upward as straight as possible.

4. Bring your knees in close to your chest.

5. Return to the starting position. Do for the specified number of seconds.

CURL-DOWN

1. Sit on the floor with your knees bent and your hands behind your head.

2. Slowly lower your upper body downward to a 45° angle or until you feel your stomach muscles begin to pull. Hold briefly.

3. Return to starting position. Do for the specified number of seconds.

LOOK-UP
(INTERMEDIATE LEVEL—ABDOMEN)

1. Lie on your back, your lower back flat on the floor, knees bent, arms crossed on your chest.

2. Curl your head and upper body upward and forward to about a 45° angle. (Be sure you curl up; don't jerk and don't arch your back.) Hold briefly.

3. Return to the starting position, and repeat for the specified number of seconds.

BICYCLE PUMPS

1. Sit with your legs extended, hands resting on the floor beside your hips.

2. Lean your upper body back slightly, and raise your legs off the floor. In this position, move your legs as though riding a bicycle. Be certain you fully extend your leg with every pump. Keep your back slightly rounded.

3. Do for the specified number of seconds.

V-SEAT

1. Sit on the floor with your legs extended and your hands on the floor next to your hips.

2. Slowly raise your legs off the floor and tilt your upper body backward slightly. Your body should form a V. (Keep your back slightly rounded.) Hold.

3. Return to the starting position. Do for the specified number of seconds.

Note: A more difficult variation is to trace a figure 8 with your feet.

CURL-DOWN

1. Sit on the floor with your knees bent and your hands behind your head.

2. Slowly lower your upper body downward to a 45° angle or until you feel your stomach muscles begin to pull. Hold.

3. Return to the starting position. Do for the specified number of seconds.

Note: This is a repetition of a beginning level exercise. You should be able to hold the curl-down position for a longer time at the intermediate level.

SIT-UPS
(ADVANCED LEVEL—ABDOMEN)

1. Lie on your back with your knees bent and arms across your chest. You may also extend your arms along your sides, or over your head, or place your hands behind your neck.

2. Curl your body up into a sitting position by first drawing your chin toward your chest and then lifting your upper body off the floor. Keep your lower back rounded throughout the movement. Sit up as far as possible.

3. Return to the starting position. Do for the specified number of seconds.

UP-OARS

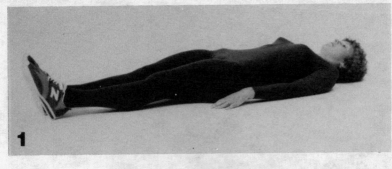

1. Lie on your back with your arms at your sides, legs extended.

2. Curl your upper body off the floor, and simultaneously bend your knees, sliding your feet toward your buttocks. Don't arch your back. When you sit up, grasp your shins.

3. Return to the starting position. Do for the specified number of seconds.

ALTERNATE TOE SPIKES

1. Lie on your back with your legs extended, arms at your sides.

2. Curl your upper body upward; as you do so, raise your left leg, and touch your right hand to your left toe.

3. Return to the starting position. Curl up again, touching your left hand to your right toe.

4. Return to the starting position. Do for the specified number of seconds.

V-SEAT WITH FLUTTER

2

3

1. Sit on the floor with your legs extended and your hands on the floor next to your hips.

2. Slowly raise your legs off the floor and tilt your upper body backward slightly. Your body should form a V. Keep your back slightly rounded.

3. Move legs up and down in a fluttering fashion. Do not let your legs touch the floor. If you have trouble maintaining your balance, move your hands behind your hips.

4. Do for the specified number of seconds.

SINGLE SIDE LEG RAISES
(BEGINNING LEVEL—WAIST)

1. Lie on your right side, your right arm extended above your head, palm against the floor, your head resting on the extended arm. Place your left hand on the floor in front of your waist for stability.

2. Raise your left leg to at least a 45° angle. Lower your leg.

3. Raise the left leg for half the specified number of seconds. Then do the exercise on your other side for half the specified number of seconds.

DOUBLE KNEE LIFTS

1. Lie on your back, arms extended at right angles to your body, palms down, knees drawn up to your chest.

2. Keeping your knees together, roll on your hips so that first your right knee touches the floor to the right of your body and then your left knee touches the floor to the left of your body.

3. Do for the specified number of seconds.

CROSSOVERS

1. Lie on your back, legs together, arms extended at right angles to your body.

2. Raise your right leg to a vertical position. Keeping your leg straight, lower it to the floor on your left side. Attempt to touch your right toe to your left hand.

3. Return to starting position. Repeat the movement with your left leg, attempting to touch your left toe to your right hand.

4. Do for the specified number of seconds.

SIDE CURL-UPS

1. Lie on your left side, arms extended in front of chest, hands about six inches in front of your hips. Have a partner hold your feet down or brace them under a piece of furniture.

2. Curl your body upward several inches. Return to starting position.

3. Do the exercise on your left side for half the specified number of seconds. Then turn and do the exercise on your right side, for half the specified number of seconds.

SIDE DOUBLE LEG RAISE
(6 INCHES)
(INTERMEDIATE LEVEL—WAIST)

1. Lie on your right side, your right arm extended above your head (palm against the floor), your head resting on the extended arm. (If you wish, you can bend your right arm and rest your head on your right hand.)

2. Keeping your legs together, raise them six inches off the floor. Lower your legs to the starting position.

3. Do for half the specified number of seconds. Then turn and do the exercise on your left side for half the specified number of seconds.

SIDE SIT-UPS

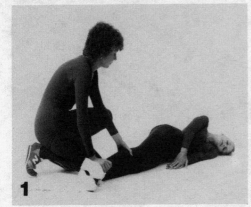

1. Lie on your left side, arms extended in front of chest, hands about six inches in front of your hips. Have a partner hold your feet down or brace them under a piece of furniture.

2. Curl your body upward as far as possible. Return to starting position.

3. Do the exercise on your left side for half the specified number of seconds. Then turn and do the exercise on your right side, for half the specified number of seconds.

SINGLE ARM AND LEG RAISE

1. Lie on your right side, your right arm extended above your head (palm against the floor), your head resting on the extended arm. Place your left hand on the floor in front of your waist.

2. Raise your left leg to at least a 45° angle. Lower your leg, and simultaneously raise your left arm. By the time your leg is down your arm should be at about a 45° angle from your body.

3. As you lower your arm, raise your leg again.

4. Do the exercise on the left for half the specified number of seconds, then on your right for half the specified number of seconds.

TWIST AND CURL-UP

1. Lie flat on your back with your knees bent, feet flat on floor, your hands placed across your chest.

2. Tighten your abdominal muscles. Curl your head and shoulders up off the floor. As you roll upward, twist slightly to the left. Hold for three seconds.

3. Return to the starting position. Do the exercise for the specified number of seconds, twisting to the alternate side each time.

SIDE SIT-UPS
(ARMS EXTENDED)
(ADVANCED LEVEL—WAIST)

1. Lie on your left side, arms extended overhead. Have a partner hold your feet down or brace them under a piece of furniture.

2. Curl your body upward as far as possible. Return to starting position.

3. Do the exercise on your left side for half the specified number of seconds. Then turn and do on the right side for half the specified number of seconds.

SIDE DOUBLE LEG RAISE
(12 INCHES)

1. Lie on your right side, your right arm extended above your head (palm against the floor), your head resting on the extended arm. (If you wish, you can bend your right arm and rest your head on your right hand.)

2. Keeping your legs together, raise them 12 inches off the floor. Lower your legs to the starting position.

3. Do for half the specified number of seconds. Then turn and do the exercise on your left side for half the specified number of seconds.

SIT-UP AND TWIST

1. Lie flat on your back with your knees bent and your hands placed behind your head.

2. Curl your body up into a sitting position by first drawing your chin toward your chest and then lifting your upper body off the floor. Keep your back rounded throughout the movement.

3. As you are completing the sit-up, twist your torso and touch your right elbow to your left knee. Then, twist to the left and touch your left elbow to your right knee.

4. Return to the starting position. Do for the specified number of seconds.

UP-OARS AND TWIST

1. Lie flat on your back with your legs extended, arms extended alongside of your body.

2. Raise your upper body off the floor and simultaneously bend your knees, sliding your feet toward your buttocks. Don't arch your back.

3. As you curl upward, twist your upper torso toward the right and also extend both arms to the right.

4. Return to the starting position. Do for the specified number of seconds, twisting to alternate sides.

LOWER BACK EXERCISES

If you are one of the millions of Americans who recoils with lower back pain after any kind of exertion—and medical authorities estimate that one out of every three Americans eventually has the problem—you know that a pain in the back is a big deterrent to any fitness program.

The back muscles are more often thought of as a source of discomfort than as a building stone toward physical fitness. Given a moderate amount of attention and exercise, however, the back muscles can be developed to a degree that will help avert most of the common back ailments. Remember, too, that the low back indirectly affects your entire figure. If you suffer from low back pain, you will be unable to do the exercises necessary to get the rest of your body in shape.

Relief of low back pain involves three steps. First, the abdominal muscles must be conditioned to provide proper balance of the pelvic girdle. Second, you must work on stretching the muscles at the back of the leg and lower back. After you have conditioned the abdominals and stretched the muscles of the leg and lower back, you can then begin doing the strengthening exercises. Be careful not to hyperextend or arch the back in the initial stages of lower back rehabilitation.

The following exercises are set up so that you'll build up your abdominals, stretch your low back muscles and hamstrings, and then strenghten the low back. Do the abdominal exercises and the stretching exercises while on Level One and Level Two. The strengthening exercises are not to be undertaken until you start Level Three. By then you will have developed adequate flexibility of the back and hamstrings and you will have sufficiently conditioned the abdominal muscles.

RELAXATION EXERCISE

1. Lie on the floor and practice relaxing the various muscle groups. Roll your head slowly from side to side.

2. Raise your left arm and let it fall to the floor. Raise your right arm and let it fall gently to the floor. Do the same thing with the legs.

3. Repeat several times.

HEAD AND SHOULDER CURL
(ABDOMINAL EXERCISES)

1. Lie on your back with your knees bent at a 90° angle, feet on the floor, hands and arms across your chest.

2. Tighten your abdominal muscles. Roll your head and shoulders up off the floor. Hold for three to six seconds.

3. Return to the starting position. Do for the specified number of seconds.

SINGLE LEG RAISE
(KNEE BENT)

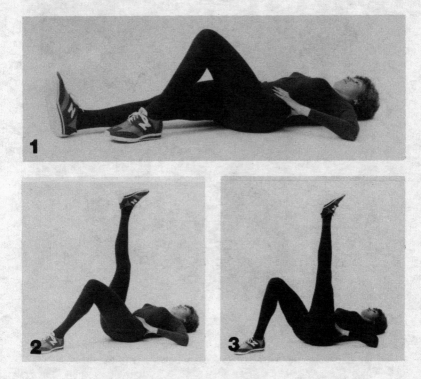

1. Lie on your back with your left knee bent and your left foot on the floor. Extend your right leg along the floor and place your hands on your hips or at your sides.

2. Raise your right leg as high as possible, keeping the small of your back against the floor. Return your right leg to the floor.

3. Do for half the specified number of seconds. Then do the exercise with your left leg for half the specified number of seconds.

KNEE TO NOSE

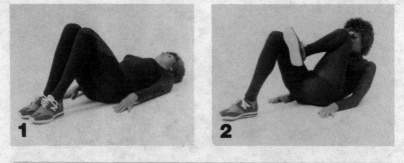

1. Lie flat on your back, knees bent, arms at sides.

2. Curl your head up and bring one knee as close to the nose as possible. Then extend the leg and let the head fall back to the resting position.

3. Do for the specified number of seconds, alternating legs.

LOOK-UP

1. Lie on your back, your lower back area touching the floor, knees bent, arms across chest.

2. Curl your head and upper body upward to about a 45° angle. (Be sure you curl up; don't jerk and don't arch your back.) Hold briefly.

3. Return to the starting position. Do for the specified number of seconds.

CURL-DOWN

1. Sit on the floor with your knees bent and your hands across the chest.

2. Slowly lower your upper body to a 45° angle or until you feel your stomach muscles begin to pull. Hold briefly.

3. Return to the starting position. Do for the specified number of seconds.

SITTING STRETCH

1. Sit on the floor with your legs extended.

2. Bending slowly at the waist, bring your head down toward the knees as close as possible. Keep the legs extended. Try to touch your toes. Hold for a few seconds. Relax.

3. Do for the specified number of seconds.

Note: Do this exercise very slowly.

SPREAD SITTING STRETCH

1. Sit on the floor with your legs spread apart.

2. Bend forward at the waist; try to bring your head as close to the floor as possible. Hold for a few seconds. Relax.

3. Do for the specified number of seconds.

Note: Do this exercise very slowly.

CAT EXERCISE

1. Kneel on your hands and knees.

2. Tighten your abdominal muscles and arch your back like an angry cat. Hold for a few seconds. Relax.

3. Do for the specified number of seconds.

PRONE LEG RAISE
(BACK STRENGTHENING EXERCISES)

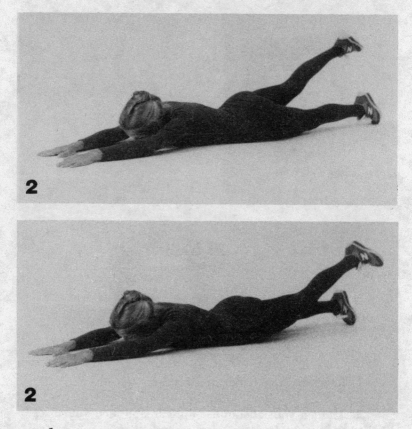

1. Lie face down on the floor with your arms extended above your head, palms resting on the floor.

2. Raise the right leg six to 10 inches off the floor. Return. Then raise the left leg.

3. Do for the specified number of seconds.

Note: Be sure to keep your chest and hips on the floor.

TWO-WAY STRETCH

1. Kneel on all fours.

2. Attempt to touch the left knee to the head. Raise your head. At the same time extend your left leg back.

3. Return to the starting position. Repeat with the other leg.

4. Do for the specified number of seconds.

HIP & DERRIERE EXERCISES

Advice to the exercise-conscious: Don't disregard your derriere! Just because you can't see your backside (except when looking in a mirror), doesn't mean you can ignore it. The gluteals, the muscles in the buttocks region, are vital to your appearance, your posture, and your energy. The gluteal muscles, or "glutes" as they are called, are the hub of the major body movements, and if yours are poorly conditioned, you'll find you tire out quickly when walking, running, or climbing.

The gluteal muscles are part of what's called the antigravity group, which also includes the thigh muscles and abdominals. Working together against the constant pull of gravity, this group of muscles allows you to stand upright. However, if one set of muscles is stronger or weaker than the others, a posture problem can result. If the gluteals aren't strong enough to offset the abdominals, the body is thrown out of line causing strain, and possibly pain, to the lower back. A person with weak gluteals is also more susceptible to sacroiliac strain when picking up heavy objects.

There are three glutes, and they are named according to their size. The gluteus maximus, the largest, overlies the other gluteal muscles. Broad and thick, it gives the buttocks their characteristic rounded shape. The gluteus maximus extends and rotates the thigh outward. You can feel the muscle move when you tense and relax the buttocks or stand up from a squatting position. You use this powerful muscle when climbing stairs or hills.

The other two muscles, the gluteus medius and the gluteus minimus, are located on the outer surface of the pelvis. They turn the hip out. It is the maximus and medius which balance the pelvis on the legs.

The buttocks should be smooth, curved, and firm. Flabby, out-of-shape gluteals, especially the maximus, tend to sag, causing a droopy derriere and, possibly, saddlebags on the thighs. To measure muscle tone, push against the buttocks when the muscles are relaxed. Then contract the muscles and push again. You should feel a great deal more resistance when the muscles are contracted. If there's little difference, start exercising.

A bulgy backside may also be due to excess fat. Use the "pinch" test to determine if this is true for you. If you do have unwanted fat, go into calorie deficit with a good daily aerobic exercise program that lasts thirty minutes or longer. Walking, jogging, and bicycling are the best aerobic exercises for the hips and derriere. Thirty minutes of this type of exercise daily will improve your muscle tone and help you attain a calorie deficit.

And stay away from girdles. This undergarment is simply a crutch meant to give you the support you should be getting from your muscles. A girdle also restricts the free flow of blood to and from the legs, causing circulation problems.

STANDING LEG EXTENSION
(BEGINNING LEVEL)

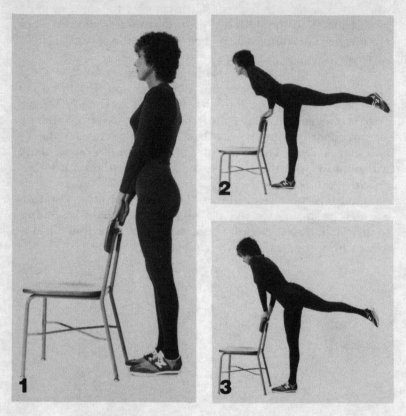

1. Stand behind a chair with both hands upon the backrest.

2. Swing one leg backward and up as high as possible. Do not arch the back.

3. Do for the specified number of seconds, alternating legs. Keep the legs straight and body erect throughout the exercise.

SIDE LEG SWINGS

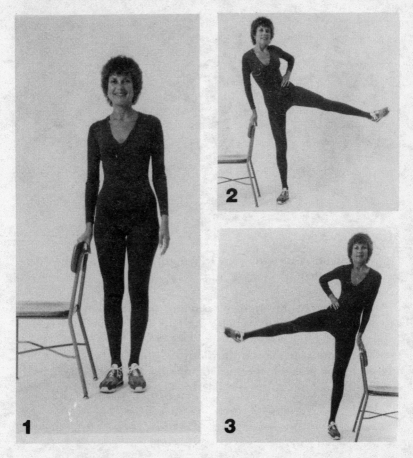

1. Stand with your right side to the back of the chair, right hand resting on the backrest.

2. Lift your left leg outward and upward as far as possible. Lower your leg.

3. Do the exercise with each leg for half the specified number of seconds. Keep your body erect and your legs straight.

SIDE STRETCH

1. Stand erect with your feet slightly more than shoulder-width apart, hands on your hips.

2. Lunge to the right by bending the right knee as much as possible, keeping the left leg straight and the body erect.

3. Return to the starting position. Repeat the exercise to the right for half the specified number of seconds, and then reverse the action to the left side for half the specified number of seconds.

DOUBLE KNEE LIFTS

1

2

1. Lie on your back, arms extended at right angles to your body, palms down, knees drawn up to your chest.

2. Keeping your knees together, roll your hips so that first your left knee touches the floor to the left of your body and then your right knee touches the floor to the right of your body.

3. Continue for the specified number of seconds.

FIRE HYDRANT
(INTERMEDIATE LEVEL)

1. Assume a kneeling position with hands on the floor.

2. Raise your left leg to the side, keeping the knee bent.

3. Straighten and extend the left leg to the side.

4. Return to the starting position. Do for half the specified number of seconds with the left leg, and then do for half the specified number of seconds with your right leg.

KNEE TO NOSE

1. Assume a kneeling position with the hands on the floor.

2. Bring your left knee in close to the chest and lower your head to meet the knee.

3. Then, extend your leg backward as far as possible. Do not arch the back.

4. Return to the starting position. Do for the specified number of seconds, alternating legs.

GLUTEAL SET

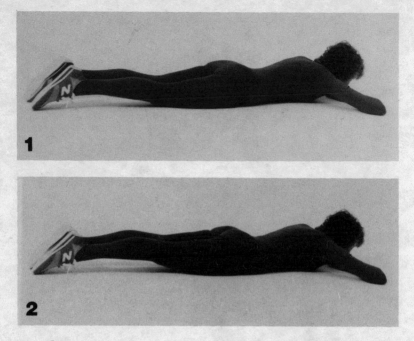

1. Lie on your stomach, chin resting on your hands, your ankles and feet together.

2. Tighten your legs and derriere muscles. Hold for a count of five. Relax. Repeat for the specified number of seconds.

SINGLE SIDE LEG RAISES

1. Lie on your right side, your right arm extended above your head (palm against the floor), your head resting on the extended arm. Place your left hand on the floor in front of your waist for stability.

2. Raise your left leg to at least a 45° angle. Lower your leg to the starting position.

3. Do the exercise on your right side for half the specified number of seconds; then do the exercise on the left side for half the specified number of seconds.

MOUNTAIN CLIMBERS
(ADVANCED LEVEL)

1. Assume a push-up position (i.e., face toward the floor, body straight and supported by hands and toes).

2. Bring your right leg up underneath the chest with the knee bent while keeping your left leg extended backward.

3. Switch position of the legs, and continue alternating fairly rapidly for the specified number of seconds.

PRONE ALTERNATE LEG LIFTS

1. Lie face down on the floor with your arms extended in front of you.

2. Tighten your derriere, and lift your right leg up as high as possible. Hold for a count of three. Relax your derriere, and lower the leg.

3. Lift alternate legs for the specified number of seconds.

Note: When you're doing this exercise, do not arch or hyperextend your back. Lift your leg with the gluteal muscles.

HIP LIFT

1. Sit on the floor, arms by your sides, knees bent, and your feet flat on the floor.

2. Raise your buttocks off the floor so that your trunk is parallel to the floor. Return to starting position.

3. Do for the specified number of seconds.

BENCH STEP

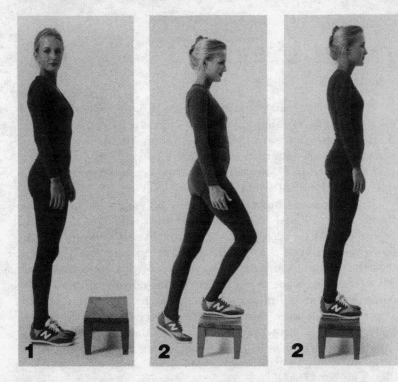

1. Stand in front of a step, sturdy stool, or a stack of newspapers tied securely together. A 12-inch height is good.

2. Step up on the bench with your right foot. Step up with your left foot. Return the right foot to the floor. Return the left foot to the floor.

3. Continue bench stepping in the manner described for the specified number of seconds.

THIGH EXERCISES

Dimples and bulges, saddlebags and cottage cheese—is there any more familiar figure problem than flabby, saggy thighs? Women of every age complain about their thighs. Their outer thighs are flabby; their inner thighs sag; they have bulges over the kneecap. No matter where they occur, fat deposits and flabby muscles result from insufficient exercise.

Firming your thighs with exercise will improve your figure. Heavy thighs can be thinned down, and thin thighs can be firmed and toned to look more attractive. If you are bowlegged, exercise will fill in and firm up your legs even though it cannot correct the basic flaw in your bone structure.

Most of us want to build up or trim down our thighs for cosmetic reasons. Firming and strengthening these muscles will also protect the knee joint, the most vulnerable joint in the body. The knee joint bears 85 percent of the body's weight; thus it is subjected to a lot of stress and is an easy target for accidents. Firming your thigh muscles will help stabilize this vital joint.

The quadriceps (four-headed) femoris is a very large muscle on the front of the thigh. It provides most of the power when you kick your leg while swimming. Some women are plagued by what appears to be flab on the inside of their knees. In reality, this "flab" is a weakened quadriceps, and it can be eliminated by strengthening the muscle.

The sartorius, also in the front of the thigh, is the longest muscle in the body. It runs diagonally from the outside of the hip to the inside of the knee. Often called the tailor's muscle, it allows you to draw one leg over the other, a characteristic posture of tailors in times past.

The adductors on the inside of the thigh draw the leg inward (adduction). The hamstrings at the back of the thigh rotate the leg outward.

The following exercises will strengthen the muscles in the

upper thigh region. If the upper muscles are strengthened, the rest of the thigh will automatically look better. Muscles work in groups; exercising the thighs also exercises the hips and derriere. To firm the muscles, do the exercises as outlined and gradually increase the length of time you spend doing them. To build up the muscles, use ankle weights while doing the exercises.

ONE-QUARTER KNEE BENDS
(BEGINNING LEVEL)

1. Stand erect with your feet close together and your hands on your hips.

2. Bend your knees to a 45° angle. As you bend, you can extend your arms forward.

3. Return to the starting position. Continue for the specified number of seconds.

WALK-HIGH KNEE ACTION

1. Walk erect with your eyes forward, chest elevated, and your shoulders and arms in a relaxed position. Your toes and heels should point straight ahead. Try to lift your knee as high as possible with every step.

2. Continue for the specified number of seconds.

QUAD SETTING

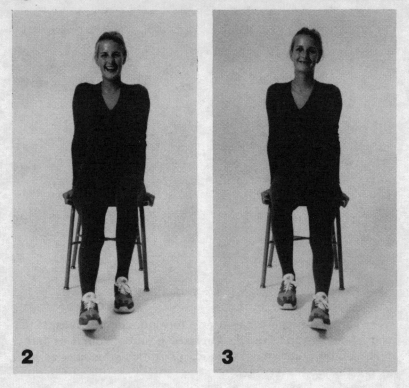

2   **3**

1. You can either sit or stand.

2. Forcibly contract the muscles at the front of the thigh by extending one leg forward and then tightening the quadriceps muscle. Hold for a few seconds. Relax.

3. Continue for the specified number of seconds, alternating legs.

FENCER'S LUNGE

1. Stand erect, feet together, left hand on your hip and the right arm extended to the side at shoulder height.

2. Take a giant stride forward with your right leg as far as possible while keeping the heel of the left foot on the floor.

3. Return. Continue to the right for half the number of seconds and then go to the left for half the number of seconds.

HALF KNEE BENDS
(INTERMEDIATE LEVEL)

1. Stand erect with your feet close together and your hands on your hips.

2. Bend your knees to a 90° angle. As you bend, you can extend your arms forward.

3. Return to the starting position. Continue for the specified number of seconds.

STRIDE HOPS

1. Stand erect with your hands on your hips or hanging loosely at your sides.

2. Kick the right leg forward and the left one rearward in a scissors fashion. Then kick the left leg forward and the right leg backward.

3. Do this exercise rapidly for the specified number of seconds.

BEAR HUG

1. Stand erect with feet comfortably apart, arms at the sides.

2. Step diagonally, taking a long stride with the right foot and swinging your arms upward at the same time.

3. Bend toward the right knee and wrap both arms around the right thigh. Keep your left foot on the floor.

4. Return to the starting position. Step with the right foot for half the specified number of seconds; then step with the left foot for half the specified number of seconds.

LEG WALL PUSH

1. Stand about 18 inches from a wall, with your back toward the wall.

2. Extend your right leg backward so that your heel is against the wall. Push backward with your right heel. Hold. Relax.

3. Repeat for half the specified number of seconds. Then do with the left leg for half the specified number of seconds.

SITTING LEG RAISE
(ADVANCED LEVEL)

1. Wear weighted shoe or heavy boot on right foot. Sit on a chair or edge of table; legs hanging over the edge.

2. Raise right leg to a horizontal position by straightening the knee. Return slowly to the starting position.

3. Do for half the specified number of seconds with weighted right foot. Then put weight on left foot, and raise left leg for half the specified number of seconds.

NO CHAIR

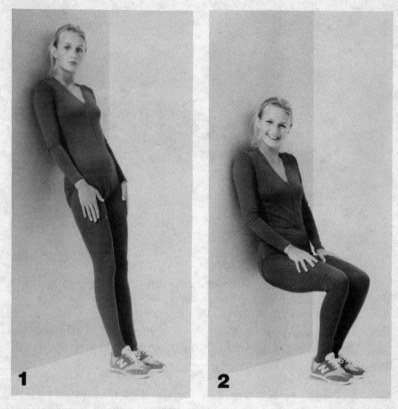

1. Lean your upper back against a wall. Your feet should be about 18 inches away from the wall. Your hands should be on your thighs.

2. Slowly slide down to a sitting position and hold for a few seconds. Return to an upright position.

3. Continue for the specified number of seconds.

KNEE CURL

1. Wear weighted shoe or heavy boot. Lie face down on the floor; hands extended above the head.

2. Curl leg upward until the weighted foot nearly or actually touches the buttocks. Slowly return to the original position.

3. Do the exercise for half the specified number of seconds with weight on right foot and for half with weight on left foot.

ONE-LEG SQUAT

1. Stand with your right side next to a wall.

2. Extend the left leg forward. Squat by bending the right leg until the upper leg and lower leg form a 90° angle.

3. Place your hand against the wall, if necessary to maintain balance. Hold this position for a few seconds.

4. Continue squats on the right leg for half the specified number of seconds. Then do squats on the left leg for half the specified number of seconds.

CALF & ANKLE EXERCISES

To have an attractively curved calf and a trim ankle, you must develop the muscles of the lower leg. To emphasize the calf's curve, you need to provide more muscle bulk. If you rise on your toes and look back at your calf, you'll see how the muscle becomes pleasantly rounded. That roundness is why high heels will always be popular, regardless of the discomfort they cause. You can develop that roundness by improving the calf muscles.

The gastrocnemius muscle forms the basis for the calf on the back of your leg. Beneath the gastrocnemius muscle is the soleus muscle. You use both of these muscles when you rise up on your toes and when you walk, run, and bicycle. On the front of the leg is the tibialis anterior muscle which allows you to flex your toe forward. All three muscles must be correctly developed to have a properly proportioned calf area.

Many women are afraid that excessive exercise will enlarge their calves, and it is true that an active person may have a larger calf than someone who is sedentary. But active people have attractive legs because, although their calves may be enlarged, their knees and ankles are trim. In contrast, sedentary people sometimes have straight legs; that is, their knees, calves, and ankles seem to run together because they are all the same thickness.

If you want to develop your calves, do the following exercises. In addition, you may want to begin a program of walking, running, or bicycling. If you decide to walk you must remember that you need more than just a leisurely walk around the house or block. Try to take a brisk, vigorous walk of 30 minutes or more every day.

TOE RAISE
(BEGINNING LEVEL)

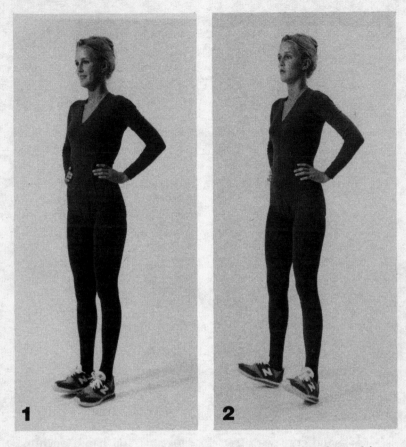

1. Stand erect with feet close together and hands on hips.

2. Raise the body up on heels as high as possible.

3. Return to the starting position. Repeat for the specified number of seconds.

HEEL RAISES

1. Stand erect with feet close together and hands on hips.

2. Raise the body up on the toes as high as possible.

3. Return to the starting position. Repeat for the specified number of seconds.

PENCIL POINTERS AND CURLS

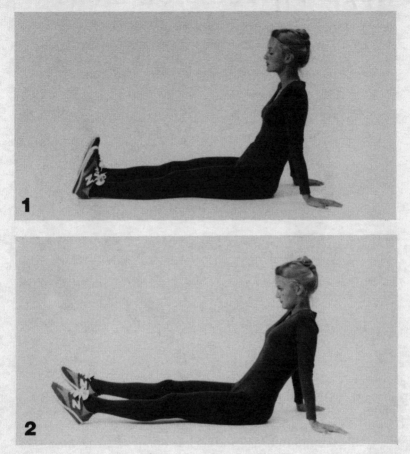

1. Sit on the floor with hands on floor, legs extended, feet about 12 inches apart.

2. Curl toes toward the face as far as possible; then point them downward as far as possible.

3. Do for the specified number of seconds.

Note: You can also alternate legs, i.e., first curl and point the right toes, then the left.

ALTERNATING SIDE KICKS

1. Stand with the elbows bent, hands held in loose fists about waist height.

2. Kick the right leg to the side about 12 to 18 inches and return; kick the left leg to the side and return.

3. Continue Alternating Side Kicks fairly rapidly for the specified number of seconds.

SINGLE HEEL RAISE
(INTERMEDIATE LEVEL)

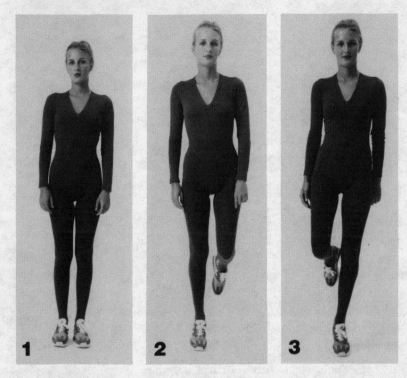

1. Stand erect with your feet together.

2. Lift the left leg slightly. Raise your body up on the right toe as high as possible. Hold for a few seconds. Relax.

3. Continue, alternating legs, for the specified number of seconds.

TOE HOP

1. Stand erect with your feet together.

2. Raise your left leg slightly. Hop lightly on the right toe about three inches off the floor.

3. Hop on the right toe for half the specified number of seconds; then hop on the left toe for half the specified number of seconds.

TOE CURL

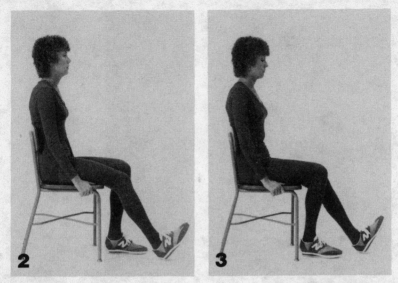

1. Sit with one leg extended.

2. Lift the toes of the extended foot while keeping the heel on the floor.

3. Continue, alternating legs, for the specified number of seconds.

ANKLE TURN

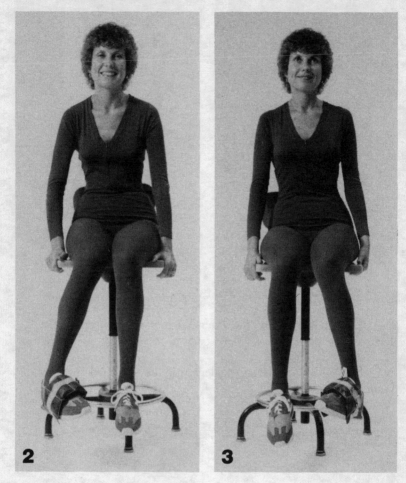

1. Wear weighted shoe or heavy boot. Sit with legs hanging.

2. Turn weighted foot inward and then outward as far as possible.

3. Continue for half the specified number of seconds. Then repeat exercise with other foot for half the specified number of seconds.

BENCH STEP
(ADVANCED LEVEL)

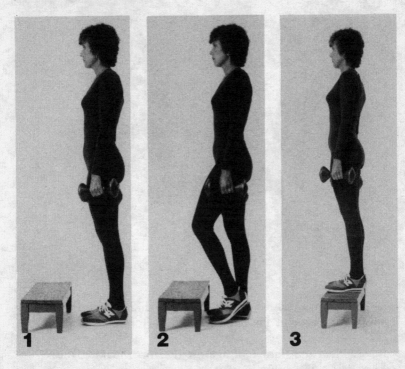

1. Stand in front of a stair step, a low bench or a stack of tied newspapers (about a 12-inch height is good). Hold 10-pound dumbbell in each hand.

2. Lift left foot onto the stair. Lift right foot onto stair. Return left foot to the floor; return right foot to floor.

3. Continue in the manner described for the specified number of seconds.

FOOT PUSH

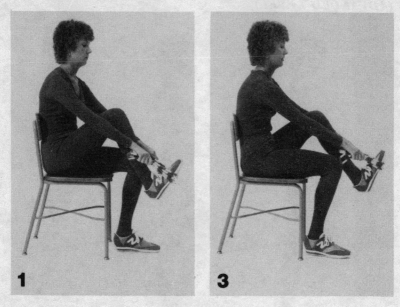

1. Sit in a chair, and lift the right thigh toward the chest. Loop a rope around the ball of the right foot.

2. Push the right foot against the rope, making the movement at the ankle joint.

3. Do the exercise using the right foot for half the specified number of seconds. Then reverse, and do using the left foot for half the specified number of seconds.

RUN IN PLACE

1. Run in place, raising the feet at least 4 inches off the floor. If you want to work harder, lift the knees higher.

2. Continue for the specified number of seconds.

HEEL RAISE WITH WEIGHTS

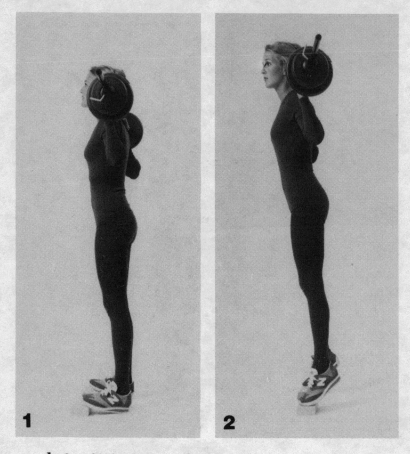

1. Stand with balls of your feet on a 1- to 2-inch block of wood (or a book); heels on floor. Hold barbell in overhand grip behind neck; the barbell should be resting on shoulders.

2. Raise up on toes as far as possible.

3. Relax. Do for the specified number of seconds.

FAT-BURNING ACTIVITY

Your body keeps a fine balance between the number of calories you eat and the number of calories that you burn off through physical activity. For example, if you take in and burn off 2,000 calories each day, your body weight will remain constant. But if you eat 2,000 calories and burn off only 1,900, you're in trouble. You will have 100 calories left over.

These extra 100 calories are converted to fat by the liver. The fat is carried to the fat cells of your body and stored. (Incidentally, your heredity determines where this fat will be deposited; you don't have much to say about that aspect of your development.) One hundred calories doesn't sound like much. But if you follow this pattern for 35 days it will amount to 3,500 calories—which is one pound of fat. If you gain one pound every 35 days, by the end of the year you'll have gained a little over ten pounds.

In summary, you gain fat when you consume more calories than you burn. And to lose fat, you must burn more calories than you consume. Therefore, there are only two ways to lose fat: eat less or move more.

EATING LESS

Dieting is the most common approach to fat loss. And *some* people can lose weight by dieting. In fact, experts say that 8 percent of the obese are able to lose weight and keep it off. But, *most* people regain the pounds they have dieted off, and sometimes it takes only a few weeks to regain what's been lost and add a few more.

Why don't diets work? One reason is that dieting isn't any fun. It requires Spartan willpower. And, judging by the 8 percent figure, most people don't have that Spartan will. Secondly, people are emotionally addicted to food. When under stress, these eating addicts stuff themselves with copious amounts of food. If their weight gains cause them to diet, they find

141

themselves under more stress. When the stress becomes acute, they go on an eating binge. And the binge causes them more upset. They are caught in a tragic cycle of stress, eating, depression, guilt, stress, more overeating, and so on.

There is an even more basic reason why some people can't keep their weight off. Dieting does not attack the basic cause of obesity—*a lack of physical activity*. Fat accumulates not so much from overeating as from underdoing.

Studies done at Harvard and other universities around the world have shown that people who are too fat generally eat no more than the lucky ones who do not have a problem with their weight. And that most people—fat and thin—eat somewhere between 2,300 and 3,000 calories a day. Studies have also shown, however, that fat people tend to exercise far less than normal weight people. In fact, some researchers have shown that the obese spend up to four times as many hours watching TV as do thin people. And fat people walk an average of 2.2 miles a day, whereas a normal weight person walks about 4.8 miles a day. That difference adds up to about twenty to twenty-five pounds a year!

MOVING MORE

As you may have already guessed, we're advocating that you move more if you want to lose weight, and we have worked a period of fat-buring exercises into the Figure Shaping Program.

There are people who say exercise isn't a very effective way of losing weight. They reason that it takes a great deal of exercise to burn off the caloric equivalent of one pound of fat. They point out, for example, that thirty-five miles of walking, seven hours of splitting wood, and eleven hours of playing volleyball are necessary to burn off one pound of fat. The flaw in this reasoning is that although the equations are true, they completely ignore the cumulative effect of exercise. Although it may take six hours of handball to burn off one pound of fat, it need not be done in a single six-hour period. One half hour of handball every day for twelve days will also burn off one pound of fat; playing handball for a year at that rate would burn twenty-five to thirty pounds. And that's a significant amount of fat!

Some critics say exercise is self-defeating; it will increase your appetite. Not so say the researchers. The appetite of an active person does increase when she starts to exercise more than usual. But, when a sedentary person increases her activity, her appetite decreases. We don't know why exercise decreases the appetite of a formerly sedentary person. The cause may be physiological, psychological, or a combination of both.

AEROBIC EXERCISE

Exercises which burn lots of calories are those that move your whole body. They involve the major muscles of your body and are performed continuously for an extended period of time. Activities such as swimming, walking, running, bicycling, and rope skipping qualify as fat-burners. They are examples of aerobic exercises.

During aerobic exercise your heart beats faster, your breathing becomes deeper, and your blood vessels expand to carry blood and oxygen to the working muscles. Your body takes in and uses more than the ordinary amount of oxygen. And using oxygen means burning calories.

When you do aerobic exercises, you use about one hundred calories every eight to twelve minutes. Aerobic activities are good calorie burners because they are continuous. For exercise to be effective in burning calories, you must keep moving from one exercise to another smoothly and without pause.

You can use all the calisthenics described in previous chapters and convert them into aerobic exercise simply by doing your push-ups in the kitchen, your v-seats in the living room, and then, if you're getting bored with the scenery, move to the dining room for single side leg raises and to the den for running in place. The point is to move and to keep moving.

Remember, the key words in describing the type of exercise to be used for removing body fat (and for improving your heart health) are "continuous," and "rhythmic," and "whole-body." Exercises that are erratic and permit stopping and starting are perhaps fine for toning muscles. But they do little to reduce your body fat or develop aerobic endurance.

HOW VIGOROUSLY?

The benefits of aerobic exercise depend upon increasing and

sustaining your heart rate. The rate at which your heart ought to beat during exercise is called your "target heart rate" and is 75 percent of your heart's maximum capacity.

Your heart's maximum capacity is the number of beats it would make per minute if your body were undergoing maximum stress. A maximum heart rate would generally be 220 beats per minute minus your age. If you are twenty years old, your maximum heart rate is 200 beats per minute. If you are sixty, it's 160 beats per minute. The formula is derived from the observation that for each year you live your heart slows down by about one beat a minute.

Although 75 percent of your maximum heart rate is the ideal exercise intensity, it's more realistic to speak in terms of your target heart rate range, which is between 70 and 85 percent of your maximum heart rate. If your heart works at below 70 percent capacity, you will achieve very little fitness benefit from the exercise unless you work at it for an extended period of time or unless you were very unfit to begin with. If your heart works above 80 percent capacity, the added benefit is negligible.

The accompanying table gives the maximum heart rate, the target heart rate, and the target heart rate range for ages twenty to seventy in five-year increments. You can calculate your own rates and range if your age falls between the increments.

When you know your target heart rate range, you can easily determine whether you are performing at the most beneficial intensity. Simply take your pulse rate at any time during the exercises. If your heart rate is in the target area, then you are doing the exercise at a proper speed. If it is too high, you should slow down.

HOW LONG?

When trying to burn calories and fat, the longer you work out the better. At rest, your energy comes from glycogen and glucose (carbohydrates). When you sprint, you're doing anaerobic exercise (an exercise that can be done literally without oxygen). Such exercise places severe stress on your body, and you get all your energy from your carbohydrate stores. But, when you perform aerobic exercise, there's a shift in your metabolism. During the first few minutes of the

YOUR TARGET HEART RATE AND HEART RATE RANGE

Maintaining your target heart rate is the key to the Figure Shaping Program. Your maximum heart rate is the greatest number of beats per minute possible for your heart. During exercise, your heart rate should be aproximately 75% of this maximum. To obtain the fat-reduction benefits of this program, maintain a heart rate between 70 and 85% of your maximum for 30 minutes.

Age	Your Maximum Heart Rate (Beats per Minute)	Your Target Heart Rate (75% of the Maximum in Beats per Minute)	Your Target Heart Rate Range (Between 70% and 85% of the Maximum in Beats per Minute)
20	200	150	140 to 170
25	195	146	137 to 166
30	190	142	133 to 162
35	185	139	130 to 157
40	180	135	126 to 153
45	175	131	123 to 149
50	170	127	119 to 145
55	165	124	116 to 140
60	160	120	112 to 136
65	155	116	109 to 132
70	150	112	105 to 128

exercise, about 90 percent of all your energy comes from carbohydrates and about 10 percent from fat. As you continue to exercise aerobically, the energy shift continues toward the utilization of more fat. After about 30 minutes, 50 percent of your energy comes from carbohydrates and 50 percent from fat. And when you go on for about two hours, 90 percent comes from fat and 10 percent from carbohydrates. The exercises you do for reducing fat should be long, steady activity; short bursts of intense activities burn only carbohydrates.

To determine the minimum amount of time you ought to spend exercising aerobically each day, first estimate your caloric imbalance. A quick way to do this is to decide how many pounds you gain (or have to struggle to keep off) each year. If five pounds is your problem, you are out of caloric balance by about 50 calories a day. If ten pounds is your problem, you are out of balance by 100 calories a day. Fifteen pounds, 150 calories. Adding a zero to your number of problem pounds will give you the approximate number of calories you are out of balance.

For every 100 calories out of balance—that is, for every ten pounds you want to lose or keep under control—you need eight to twelve minutes of exercise per day at target heart rate levels.

HOW OFTEN?

Now that you know how long and how hard, the next question is how often should you exercise each week? We recommend that you exercise a minimum of four times a week. Exercising three days a week is not enough to make fast changes.

OUR FAT-BURNING PROGRAM

Our Figure Shaping Program includes walking and running as fat-burning activity. The only equipment necessary to perform these activities is a good pair of running shoes. If you wish, and you find it convenient, you can bicycle, swim, or go cross-country skiing instead. Just remember that you must keep moving for the specified time at your target heart rate level.

At Level One you will get your body into the rhythm of weight control with a program of brisk walks. A brisk walk is not a leisurely stroll. You have to get out there and step lively to get full benefit of the program. At Stage One, you should walk for fifteen to sixteen minutes. As your physical condition improves, you can move to Stage Two, where you will walk for seventeen to nineteen minutes. When you are no longer challenged by that amount of activity, move to Stage Three and continue in this manner through Level One. As you progress, you might also try more challenging walks; for example, walk faster or walk uphill.

In Level Two, Stage Seven, you add running to your walking program. When doing the run sequence try a fifty-fifty ratio of walking to running. The "telephone pole maneuver" is an easy way to keep track of your distance. That is, walk a telephone pole, jog a telephone pole. As you progress from stage to stage, you increase the amount of time you spend running and reduce the amount of time you walk. But don't be a slave to this principle. Remember, you can achieve the same benefit by walking. It's just that you can make your exercise a bit more efficient by interspersing it with some jogging.

By the time you reach Level Three, Stage Thirteen, you probably will have lost a lot of body fat and you'll like what you see in the mirror. Your figure will be returning to a glory you thought was gone forever. In Level Three, you spend more time running than walking. You can still use the telephone pole maneuver, as long as you keep your body moving. (See our chart on page 20-21.)

APPENDIX:
WARM-UP/COOL-DOWN EXERCISES

These are exercises to be done before and after each exercise session in the Figure Shaping Program. They will loosen the muscles, tendons, and ligaments of your legs, neck, and shoulders. When done before the workout, they will prepare your body for the more vigorous exercises to come. When done after, they will slow your body down and prepare it for normal activity.

For the warm-up before you exercise, do these exercises in the order they appear. After you exercise, cool down by doing them in reverse order. Take ten to twenty seconds for each exercise. Pace yourself so that you enjoy your warm-ups and cool-downs.

WALL PUSH-UP

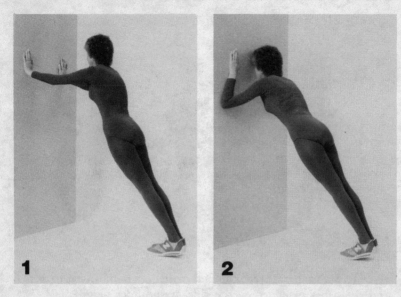

1. Stand about three feet away from a wall. Place both hands on the wall at shoulder height.

2. Keeping your body rigid, slowly bend your arms and touch your chin to the wall. (Take three seconds.)

3. Push away from the wall until your arms are straight. (Take three seconds.) You will have returned to the starting point.

4. Repeat for 10 to 20 seconds.

FENCER'S LUNGE

1. Stand erect, feet together, with left hand on your hip and the other extended to the side at shoulder height.

2. Take a giant stride forward with your right leg as far as possible while keeping the heel of the left foot on the floor. (The stride should be sufficient for a "pull" to be felt on the calf of the left leg.) Hold for a few seconds.

3. Repeat on the other side, and continue for 10 to 20 seconds.

ONE-QUARTER KNEE BENDS

1. Stand erect with your feet close together and hands on your hips.

2. Bend your knees to a 45° angle. As you bend, you can extend the arms forward.

3. As you start to feel a "tug" on your calf, hold for a few seconds. Return to starting position.

4. Repeat for 10 to 20 seconds.

SIDE LEG STRETCH

1. Stand erect with your feet slightly more than shoulder-width apart. Hands on your hips.

2. Bend the right knee as far as possible, keeping the left leg straight and the trunk erect.

3. Hold for a few seconds. Return to the starting position.

4. Repeat on the other side. Continue for 10 to 20 seconds.

TOE RAISES

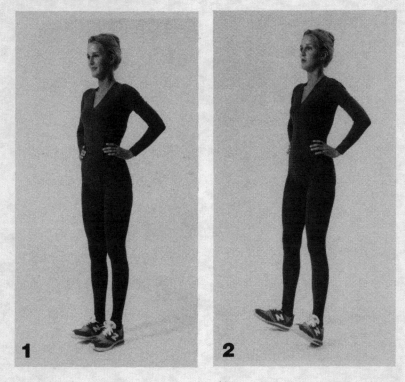

1. Stand erect with the feet close together and hands on the hips.

2. Raise your toes off the floor, placing your weight on the heels. Hold for a few seconds. Return to starting position.

3. Repeat for 10 to 20 seconds.

MOUNTAIN CLIMBERS

1. Assume a push-up position (i.e., face toward the floor, body straight and supported by hands and toes.)

2. Bring your right leg up underneath the chest with the knee bent while keeping left leg extended backward.

3. Switch position of the legs, and continue alternating fairly rapidly for 10 to 20 seconds.

KNEE TO NOSE

2

3

1. Lie flat on your back, knees bent, arms at sides.

2. Curl your head up and bring one knee as close to your nose as possible. Hold for the specified number of seconds. Then extend the leg and let your head fall back to its resting position.

3. Repeat with other leg. Continue for 10 to 20 seconds.

CAT EXERCISE

1. Kneel on your hands and knees.

2. Tighten your abdominal muscles and arch your back like an angry cat. Hold for a few seconds. Relax.

3. Do for 10 to 20 seconds.

SITTING STRETCH

1. Sit on the floor with your legs extended.

2. Bending slowly at the waist, bring your head down toward the knees as close as possible. Try to touch your toes. Hold for a few seconds. Relax.

3. Repeat for 10 to 20 seconds.

Note: Do this exercise very slowly.

SPREAD SITTING STRETCH

1. Sit on the floor with your legs spread apart.

2. Bend forward at the waist; try to bring your head as close to the floor as possible. Hold for a few seconds. Relax.

3. Repeat for 10 to 20 seconds.

Note: Do the exercise very slowly.

HEAD FLEXOR

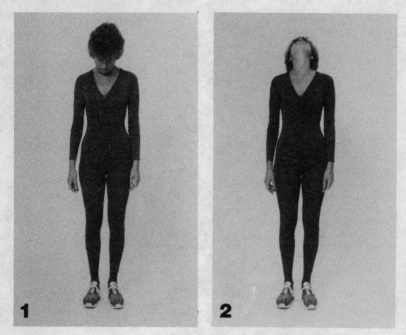

1. Standing with your arms at your sides, flex your head forward by dropping your chin to your chest. Try to draw your chin down as far as possible.

2. Extend your head backward as far as possible. Relax.

3. Repeat for 10 to 20 seconds.

NECK TURNS

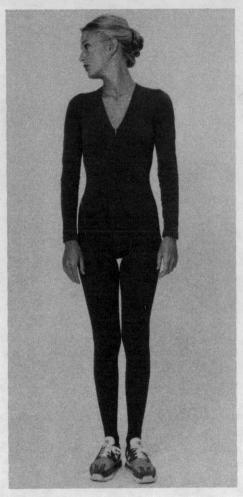

1. Stand with your arms at your sides. Turn your head to the right, and look over your right shoulder.

2. Turn your head to the left, and look over your left shoulder.

3. Continue for 10 to 20 seconds.